A Captive Freed
A Captive Made

An Autobiography

Peter C. Horrell

Ark House Press
arkhousepress.com

Some names and identifying details have been changed to protect the privacy of individuals.

Cataloguing in Publication Data:
Title: A Captive Freed A Captive Made
ISBN: 978-1-7645620-7-2 (pbk)
Subjects: REL012170 RELIGION / Christian Living / Personal Memoirs.

Design by initiateagency.com

With thanks to:

The Plummer Family
Mr & Mrs E.A. & G.E. Plummer.
Peter, Margaret, Doug, and Richard
Without whom this would never have been written.

And to Tiffany Francis, thank you for your invaluable input.

Contents

Preface

Over the years my family and friends have asked me to write something about my life. I have always been reluctant to do so. The thought of writing about myself has never sat comfortable with me as it seemed to me it would be a self-centred thing to do. I have never liked being the centre of attention preferring to remain in the shadows, rather than being in the spotlight, besides, I really had no interest in doing so. As far as I was concerned my past was in the past and I do not like digging up old bones.

At the time of writing, I am in my 90th year, and I've had a change of mind for two reasons. The first is that I have 3 children, and 5 grandchildren, who know nothing of my background. They know nothing about my past life. It's a blank. So, I now feel that to leave a written account of my life for them, 'warts and all' is important. The second is that I want to show what God has accomplished in my life and, in doing so, to glorify to His name. This is the story of my life but, of far more importance, it is the story of God's unending love in reaching out and calling me to Himself. I write my story as a testimony to His love.

Conquered, at last my life I gave,
A captive freed, yet a captive made;

He freed me from my chains of vice,
I'm still a slave, but the slave of Christ;
Held forever in God's embrace,
Forever imprisoned in His realm of grace.

Peter C. Horrell

Birth

How to begin? Well, I was born in the year of the RAT according to the Chinese Zodiac. And, according to Dr. Google, the fount of all knowledge, it was a leap year too. There was a full moon shining over the city of Bristol where I was born. Anyway, that's what Google reveals about 10th of January 1936. It also reveals I was born into the Silent Generation. Well, I don't know about that; whether I was silent at the time I came into this world I'll never know!

XC 360722

CERTIFICATE OF BIRTH

Name and Surname Peter Clarence Horrell

Sex Boy

Date of Birth Tenth January 1936 6-40 pm

Place of Birth — Registration District: Bristol

Sub-district: Ashley.

Certified to have been compiled from records in the custody of the Registrar General. Given at the General Register Office, Somerset House, London, under the Seal of the said Office, the 19 day of August 1971.

XC 360722 is the number on my birth certificate, a square 15cm piece of pink paper.

Full Name and Surname: Peter Clarence Horrell.
Sex: Boy.
Date of Birth: Tenth January 1936. **Time:** 6.40 pm.
District: Ashley. **City:** Bristol.
Country: England.

The original is somewhere in Somerset House, London which states "father unknown." I was born a nobody.

Ashley? Ashley, in Bristol, was a Salvation Army Maternity Hostel for unwed mothers. The name Clarence? Whoever gave me that moniker, and why, I don't know. The name sounded posh, upper-class. There is a "Clarence House" in London, the residence for members of the Royal Family. I wonder? ... No, no, surely not someone from ...

When I was a teenager, I used to fantasize about my unknown father as being some wealthy aristocrat, rich and living in a large stately country mansion. I imagined myself discovering who he was and paying him a visit. I would knock on his mansion door and say, "surprise, surprise Daddy, I'm your long-lost son so, let's begin to get to know each other by first opening that fat wallet of yours."

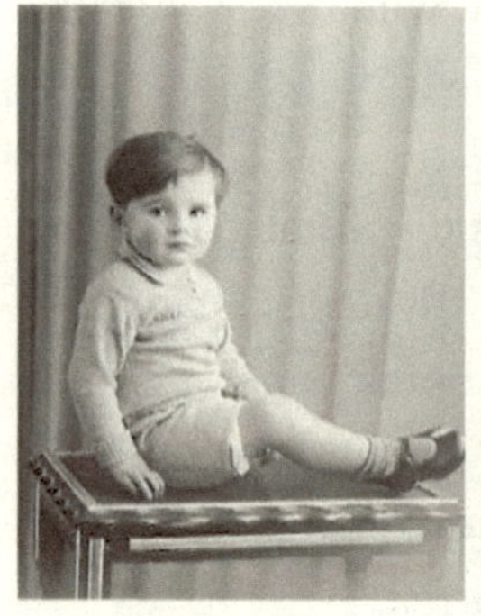

Peter

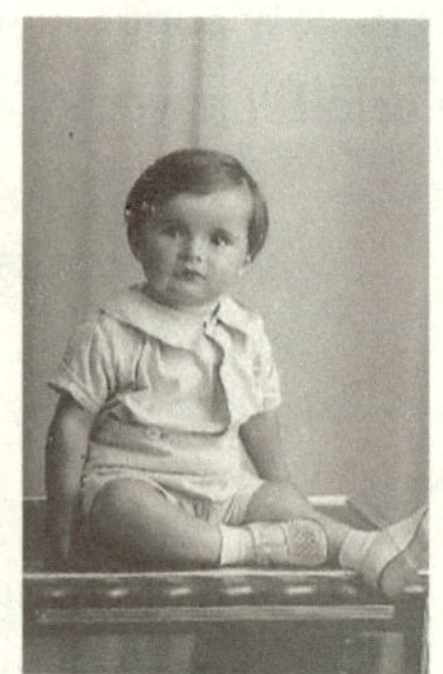

John

Later in life I learned I was a twin. His name was John. He died from encephalitis at fifteen months. When things got tough for me later in my life, I thought he was the lucky one. I saw an old brown photograph of us sitting side by side on an old-fashioned cushioned seat. Where it was taken, and by whom, I have no idea. In the past to be born out of wedlock always carried a stigma. Not anymore.

St. Vincent's Orphanage

My very first memory of life is of being held in the arms of a nun. Strange that that is my first memory of life. I was in St. Vincent's Orphanage, Torquay, Devon, UK, run by the "Sisters of Mercy." This was to be my home from 1936 to 1943, the first seven years of my life.

St. Vincents was a spooky place. During my time there I had bad dreams and nightmares of being chased through its underground cellars by ghosts with no way of escape, they were vivid dreams that left me terrified. The nuns were generally kind but one or two were harsh in their treatment of us; for example, if you wet your bed it was followed by a thrashing.

St. Vincents Orphanage. Torquay, Devon, UK
A Place of Horrors.

It was war time and Torquay was in the firing line of the German bombers on their way to bomb the naval ports in Plymouth. I vaguely remember the barrage balloons floating high in the sky, the search lights scanning the skies for German aircraft, the sound of the sirens, and I remember hearing the distinct drone of German bombers as they flew overhead. When the air raids took place, we were all quickly ushered by the nuns into the deep cellars of the orphanage for safety. I can still hear the muffled explosives of bombs going off and feel the earth tremble whilst the nuns sought to comfort and protect us through their prayers. It is still clear in my memory to this day.

One day I was taken to Mother Superiors' office. She told me a lady was going to take me away. Though I was very young I sensed Mother Superior's concern reaching out to me. I will never forget her; she had a very kind face. The lady who came to take me away turned out to be my mother. I was seven, and it was the first time I can ever remember meeting her. She took me to the small town of Okehampton in Devon.

(St. Vincent's Orphanage, established in 1889 no longer exists. It was closed in 1982 its buildings demolished, and its records tucked away, and hidden somewhere deep in the archives of the Vatican out of sight and out of mind.)

OKEHAMPTON

I discovered I had a family. I had a grandfather and a grandmother, I had aunties, uncles, cousins, and a half-sister named Freda. Like me, she did not know who her father was either. They were living in what was then the small town of Okehampton. This township was to become the centre in my life. Whenever I am asked where I come from, I still reply, Okehampton. In the beginning I felt surrounded by strangers but over time I began to feel more at home.

OKEHAMPTON 1943-1944
A Place of Surprises

The war was still on and "ration books" were still in use, limiting the amount of food one could purchase. There were many shortages. I remember having to stir oxo cubes in hot water in which I dipped my dry bread. When a loaf of bread was cut, the slices were very thin so the loaf could last longer.

Then it all suddenly came to an end. After less than about 6 months I was taken away. I remember being on a train with my mother. I remember being left all alone in a large room. I remember being frightened and bawling my eyes out. I did not know where I was. I had been abandoned into the care of a Dr. Barnardo's Home for homeless boys. I was seven or eight and that place would be my home for the next six years.

I often thought back and wondered why I was made to leave Okehampton. Even though the war was drawing to its close, they were still difficult times in which to live. The house there was crowded, things were scarce. The only thing I can think of is that the family thought I could be better looked after by the welfare authorities.

I didn't really get to know my new-found family. It was only later in life that I got to know them more intimately. I wasn't given enough time to get to know my sister Freda, and it would be about six years before I saw her again. There were two aunts with whom I bonded from the beginning. Aunt Eva and Ada were very protective of me. Later in life, whenever I visited Okehampton they were the very first I would visit.

Dr. Barnardo's Home

New Lodge, Windsor Forest, Windsor, Berks. 1944-1950
A Place of Happiness

About 10-12 years old

New Lodge was first used as a royal hunting Lodge in 1857. It was sold in 1942 and became a Dr. Barnardo's Home for boys between the ages of five to fifteen. Dr Barnardo was a pioneer in social work in the 19th century during which time he founded more than ninety homes for homeless children. He had been preparing to go as a missionary to China but felt compelled to remain in England to help homeless children.

I began to respond to the warmth and love of my carers. The first surprise I got was being able to choose sweets and lollies off a trestle table every Sunday morning after church. The first time I just gawked at all the lollies not knowing what I was supposed to do. One of the carers came to my aid, picked up some sweets, and handed them to me. What a treat!

Dr. Barnardo required that all the boys and girls under his care attend church every Sunday. So, every Sunday morning, we paraded before the Lodge and, in single file, walked to All Saints Church about a quarter of a mile away. I remember the ancient church with its pews, dark with age, and as hard as rock to sit upon. I can't remember receiving any spiritual enlightenment from what the vicar had to say, probably because we were fidgeting and giggling in the back pews.

New Lodge was situated in wide open country. With other boys I climbed trees, 'scrumped' (pinched) apples from nearby orchards and got myself into mischief on many occasions. We were well cared for at the Lodge. I particularly liked the rabbit stew with dumplings we often had for supper. There were billiard tables where we could play billiards or snooker with our carers. Once a month, on a Saturday evening, we watched black and white films of Tarzan, played by Johnny Weissmuller, in the main Hall. We also saw the funny antics of Charlie Chaplin that made us all laugh.

I attended a mixed school close to Windsor Castle. I think it may have been called St. George's School, Windsor. I was not a good student. On the contrary I was a very poor student, more interested in play, and getting into mischief than in learning the three "R's': Reading, Writing, and 'Rithmetic.

Windsor Castle was *my* castle. It was *my* playground. Back in the 1940's I was able to do what very few modern-day schoolboys can possibly do today. I have very happy memories of running alone through the castle's long corridors and passing through its stately rooms. I think I may have even sat on the King's Throne in the Throne Room. I climbed the steep steps and was able look down from the White Tower's high turrets to the streets below. And I was a schoolboy, all alone! Who could do that today?

During the school holidays, we went by train down to Cornwall staying in the township of Marazion overlooking St. Michael's Mount. The only way to walk across to the Mount itself was at low tide. I liked to try to be the first to cross the causeway by wading up to my waist to do so. I also remember seeing a large battleship leaning hard against rocks near the shore. Years later, I learned it was the famous battleship HMS *Warspite*, renowned for its service during World War 1.

The time I spent at Dr. Barnardo's Home in Windsor were happy days, but they were coming to an end. I was fifteen. It was time to leave the safety, the love, and the security of New Lodge and my carers, and venture alone into the unknown world.

(*On a trip from Australia to England in the 80s my wife and I visited New Lodge. It's still a stately old lodge but no longer a Dr. Barnardo's Home. In our search for "All Saints Church" we discovered only the site on which it once stood. It had been demolished*)

Bristol

1951-1954

I was put on a train and told my mother would meet me at the station upon my arrival. I cannot remember her ever visiting me during the six years at Barnardo's Home and I didn't not know where I was going. It turned out to be Bristol, where I had been born. When we met, I can't remember any warm embrace from my mother, and for the remainder of her long life there was always that distance between us.

She was a heavy drinker, smoker, and an alcoholic. With her female friends she would go out in the evenings and return late at night under the influence of drink. I always felt uncomfortable in the presence of her friends whom she would invite home after a night of drinking. I always shied away from them.

(During my last visit to Britain from Australia in the 90s, just before her death, my mother read a poem she had written about my twin brother John in which she revealed her loss for him. I often have wondered why she did so in my presence. When the rest of the family heard what she had done they were outraged.)

Most evenings I spent alone as I had no friends my own age with whom I could connect. As a teenager I was self-conscious, shy, and preferred to keep to the shadows rather than be the focus of people's attention. I cringed when anyone asked me about myself. I would become tongue-tied and feel foolish. I lacked self-confidence, a trait that would stay with me into adulthood. Another disadvantage I had as a 16-year-old was being small in stature. I looked much younger than my actual age which prevented me from being able to see A rated movies such as Dracula or Frankenstein.

The Childhood Welfare Dept had arranged for me to start work on a sport's ground belonging to WD & HO WILLS TOBACCO FACTORY in Bristol. This was to be my introduction into the world of sport. Football, rugby, hockey, cricket, tennis, and bowls were all played here, and over time I become an avid player of cricket and tennis. I joined a team of five groundsmen who looked after the grounds. Two of them had experienced the horrors of war. One of them suffered the terrible effects of gas used during the 1st World War. The other had lost an eye and half his face in the 2nd World War. His tank was hit by a German shell and he was the sole survivor of his tank crew.

There are things that tend to stand out when looking back on one's younger days. To get to work I used to take a short-cut from home by walking along the middle of the railway tracks. This was common practice back in the 50's. Nothing much in those days seemed to be off limits when compared with the strict rules, and safety standards of today. The oncoming express trains thundering along the track had no intention of slowing down. With their long blasting horns warning you to get off the track they would roar past almost blowing you over. No way in this wide, wide world was the engine driver going to slow down as you walked beside the track.

There was another incident, or accident, that I well remember. It took me a long time to save up and buy myself a second-hand bicycle so I could ride rather than walk to work. One afternoon, returning home, I was racing down the Bristol Hill Road at a speed only a 16-year-old would dare to do when a vehicle swerved in front of me sending me somersaulting over its handlebars. In those days crash-helmets for cyclists were never heard of. There were shouts and screams as people rushed across the street to my aid. I was completely unhurt, and to this day I still don't know how I landed on my feet without a scratch.

Although I was working for a Tobacco Company, it never crossed my mind to smoke. I was living at home where the air was always thick with tobacco smoke. My mother was addicted to both smoking and drinking. Little did I know I was to go down the same destructive road in later years.

I took a liking to reading and began to foster an increasing love for books. As I look back, I think that was the first step to what I call 'self-educating.' I became an avid reader and loved ancient history, archaeology, geography, Greek mythology, and fiction. My favourite author of fiction was Edgar Wallace who wrote the series, "The Four Just Men." I also liked reading the adventures of Detective Dick Tracy, Special Agent, and the tough giant Garth, printed in the comic strips of the daily newspapers. Oddly enough, I took a special interest in reading about Africa, known as the Dark Continent, not knowing that one day I would wind up spending some time there.

At the age of eighteen I received a registered OHMS telegram informing me to report to military H/Q to serve my two years of National Service in the army. This was an invitation from His Majesty, the King, and to refuse to go you would see you in one of his prisons.

I said farewell to my friends on the Sportsground who, in turn, wished me the very "best of British luck."

1st Battalion Gloucestershire Regiment. Company photo – Training Camp, Gloucestershire. Sitting first row far right

National Service
1954-1956

The very first thing I received upon my arrival at the Army Training Camp was a haircut; short back and sides, and very short! In the 50's the popular hair style among young men was a DA (Ducks Arse) because from the back that's what it looked like, a DA. It was popular with the "Teddy Boys" of the day and took a long time to prim and trim to perfection. It was never my own style. Lining up outside the barber's I could hear pleas coming from inside, asking the army barber not to cut too much off, but all to no avail. Their DA's were shorn off leaving behind only skinned heads.

We then lined-up to be issued with our army kit. First the kit bag that held our army uniform, hob-nailed boots, socks, underwear, helmet, mess tins and eating utensils, plus a 303 Enfield rifle (unloaded). Later we were given a metal 'dog tag' with our eight-digit service number, stamped into it. These 'dog tags' were issued in case you accidently stepped on a land mine, or had a bomb come down squarely on your head. Your 'dog-tag' would survive the blast and would serve as proof to your dear old Granny, or Mummy, that you had indeed been blown to kingdom come, or to that other place! When first given my eight-digit service number I wondered how I could ever remember it. I'm now of an old age, and if I forget the date of my birth, I'll know I'm losing some of my marbles. However, if I ever forget my service number, **23020010**, then I'll know I've lost the lot!

Army life was 'spit and polish.' Our own spit, our own polish. The toecaps of our boots had to be rubbed smooth, polished and made to shine so the sergeant major could see a reflection of his own face in them. Brasso was used to shine our brass buttons, belt fittings, and badges, that had to sparkle. I remember one dress parade I was on when the Sargent Major was inspecting me. As he slowly looked up and down at my uniform, he turned his face close to mine and shouted, "bum fluff!." Apparently, my cheeks had on them what he called bum fluff. Up until then, I had no need to shave but from that day on I had to.

Belts and gaiters had to be squeaky-clean; no hair allowed on your face or on the back of your head. If you failed an inspection on dress parade, and there were many, you were put on a 'charge,' meaning extra guard duty. Those who balked against this army discipline soon found themselves as guests of His Majesty in one of the toughest military prisons in England. These military prisons were renowned for holding the "hard cases;" i.e., those who refused to obey army orders. The only ones who were more of a hard case than the hard cases who were jailed were the army wardens guarding them. Believe me, they were not 'mummies' boys.

Basic training was tough, very tough, and there was no let-up. There were forced route marches, in full battle gear, over long distances that had to be completed in double quick time. To fall short of that time resulted in a good bawling out by our sergeant, and again the prospect of extra guard duty. When on guard duty we were armed with heavy pick handles to ward off any potential attack on the camp by the Irish Republic. If attacked, our orders were simple; "give 'em such a hard whack under the left ear so they don't wake up in hospital for at least twenty-four hours!"

During basic training I learned how to shoot, how to take apart, and quickly put back together a Bren gun, how to toss grenades, and how to fight in unarmed combat. Basic training also involved bayonet charging toward straw bodies representing men, always aiming for the heart. Our sergeant emphasized the importance of keeping our rear end down when crawling toward the enemy. He should know, he learned the hard way as he was shot up the backside during the Korean War.

Swearing is part and parcel of barrack room language. I cannot remember when I first swore, it just seemed to become part of my vocabulary. Although I must have learned just about every swear word in the Devil's dictionary, I never used the Lord's name in vain. It never, ever entered my head to do so. On drill parades our regimental Sergeant Major used the name of Jesus in the foulest manner. It was blasphemy at its worst, and even though I was not religious, I knew it was wrong. *(Years later I learned this Sergeant Major was found guilty, court-martialled and imprisoned for serious offences against recruits).*

There were some non-smokers in the army back in the 50s. but I was not one of them. I can't remember my first cigarette, but somewhere along the way I became addicted, getting through an easy thirty Woodbines a day. Woodbines were the cheapest and one of the most popular brands of cigarettes in Britain. We got them even cheaper in the NAAFI.

Upon finishing my three-month training course, our C Company marched to Scarborough, about 220 miles, where we lived under canvas for another nine months of military exercises. It was also the depot for storing some of the army's gasoline. There was a massively high stack of jerry cans just outside camp that we had to take turns in guarding. The IRA would have loved to have put a lighted match to the lot just to enjoy the fireworks and watch us running around, lit up like roman candles.

As a smoker I had my own lighter. The type of lighter back in the 50's that was stuffed with cotton wool and that had to be soaked in petrol every now and again to keep it working. We took turns in being put on guard duty, and, upon hearing that a mate was going on duty, I asked him if he could top up my lighter. A couple of hours later I saw him holding a burnt hand, running between two military guards under arrest. He did fill my lighter and then, to see if it worked, flicked it. It worked. He got a good dressing down and extra guard duty. Fortunately, the burns were not too deep.

After about 10 months we marched the 110 miles from Scarborough to Yorkshire, again in full battle dress, where we were to be stationed at the bleak and cold town of Barnard Castle. Come hail, snow, bitter cold, and numbed fingers on the freezing Yorkshire Moors, there was no let-up in our training, nor in having to turn out for dress parade. Dress parades still took place, and our turnout had to be immaculate. We lived in prefabricated Nissen huts with a stove set in the centre to supply heat. That stove glowed red hot as we fed it constantly with coke throughout the freezing days and nights.

When allowed to go on leave, I would board the "Flying Scotsman" at York with three mates and head south at high-speed thundering along the tracks non-stop until we reached Bristol. The "Flying Scotsman" is an icon and is the most famous steam locomotive in the world. It is a masterpiece of engineering and has travelled on different railways around the world.

Reports began circling around the camp that our regiment was going to be sent overseas but the location was anyone's guess. Was it to be Northern Ireland where the IRA were fighting for their independence? Was it to be Cyprus to protect the Greeks from the Turks? Was it to be in the jungles of Malaya? The answer finally came when we exchanged our heavy winter uniforms for jungle greens suited for jungle warfare. Our regiment was heading to Kenya, East Africa, where the Mau Mau were savagely slicing up their victims with their cane knives, known as pangas.

Our troop ship, the HMS *Halladale*, slowly pulled away from Liverpool Docks to a recording of Vera Lynn singing her famous and tear-jerking song: *"We'll Meet Again, Don't Know Where, Don't Know When"* blaring out from the dock's loudspeakers. On the dock parents, wives, and girlfriends were sobbing and waving their goodbyes with white hankies as our ship slowly pulled away. I was on top deck with three close friends whom I would like to mention. There was Bill (Willie) Bennett, Stan Dyer, and Farmer. We never knew Farmer's christian name but, as he worked on a farm before being called up, we simply nick-named him Farmer. We were called up together; we would be demobbed together and, in between, share danger and pub crawls with lots of laughs along the way.

An infantry regiment is normally comprised of about 800 men, so we were packed together like sardines on board the troopship and below deck we slept in hammocks. As we sailed into warmer waters, we spent most of the time on deck dressed only in shorts. It was time to go native and get a good tan on our lily-white bodies. Physical training took place daily to keep us fit and frisky, ready for action. Films were shown on top deck throughout the voyage to help pass the time, while below deck, men played cards, gambling with what money they had. I joined them once and earned some good cash.

As our Ship passed slowly through the Suez Canal the locals wildly shook their fists at us while others were giving us what looked like the Italian Salute, i.e., the middle finger. They were shouting at us in Arabic with what I presumed were some colourful swear words. One local dropped his baggy slacks and turned his bare backside towards us. I got the distinct impression he wanted us to kiss it. Now-a-days we call this being "mooned."

While sailing through the Red Sea I saw something in the sky that continues to baffle me to this present day. It was a clear night, and I was on top deck where a film was being shown. I just happened to look up and saw high above three small dots of lights moving in formation at an extraordinary speed across the clear sky. One was ahead and two behind side by side as if following its leader. There was no sound of any aircraft and before I could call my friend, Willie, they were out of sight. I still have no explanation for what I had seen that evening.

When our ship docked in Aden, today known as the People's Democratic Republic of Yemen, we were allowed to go ashore. It was a shabby, dark and poverty ridden place where prostitution was rife. Invitations to enjoy the pleasures of the 'ladies of the night,' came thick and fast from the locals but during our basic training we had been given lectures about sexually transmitted diseases such as gonorrhoea and syphilis. Slides were shown depicting the male's private parts and the awful effects of these diseases. Just watching these images made us cringe and cross our legs. We joked and laughed, making crude jokes to each other about what we were seeing. After the lecture we uncrossed our legs, but the final message of the army medical doctor got through to us. "Take my word for it, lads," he said, "don't touch these ladies even with a sanitized forty-foot barge pole."

Back in the 50's the 'cosh' was the popular defence toy of the day. It consisted of a heavy lead ball wrapped in a pretty piece of coloured cloth attached to the wrist by a cord. It was part of the standard dress carried by self-respecting Teddy Boys. They felt naked without it. When our ship stopped at different ports, the locals would come along side in their boats laden with their merchandise, and coshes were in high demand. We were not allowed off the ship so, the only way to get what you wanted was to first toss down your money, and they would throw what you wanted up to you. We had to do a lot of running and ducking for cover when coshes landed around us with their dull clunk on top deck.

As our ship passed through the Gulf of Aden into the Indian Ocean, the upper and lower decks became awash with vomit. The swells of the ocean caused many to succumb to seasickness. The swells of the ocean were very high, and the smells even higher. There were green and pale faces all around the ship. I thought I had already heard the full vocab of swear words until then. My friend, Farmer, who wouldn't say boo to a goose, was cursing every politician, including the Prime Minister, dear old Winnie, for having the audacity to send him to this god-forsaken land of Africa. I still smile at the memory of seeing my old friends' white face and gangling figure staggering towards me cursing every member of Parliament.

Kenya, East Africa

About four weeks after we left Liverpool we arrived at our destination, the Port of Mombasa, Kenya, where we disembarked. The first thing I noticed was the pure white sandy beaches. As far as I could remember, I cannot recall ever seeing a pure white beach at home. As we were hanging about to board a train for the next leg of our journey an officer, whom I knew, jokingly said to me, 'Peter Horrell, we'll bury you in this land.' It was said in jest. Sadly, he was the one who was buried in Kenya. A group of officers and been drinking, and on their return to camp their army Rover crashed, and he lost his life.

With our kitbags on our shoulders, we boarded a very long open carriage train to travel the 450-mile journey north to the town of Nakuru where the British army had its headquarters. As our train slowly drew into camp another train was slowly pulling out with the Scottish regiment, the Black Watch. They had just finished their term in Kenya, and we were taking their place. It also made sense that, as we arrived, they should leave. Having two different regiments in the same camp was a recipe for a punch-up. Fist fights between two different regiments inevitably leave behind black eyes, loose teeth, and swollen lips. All great fun!

Before our first patrol our 303 Enfield rifles were exchanged for a shorter version which had a flash eliminator, enabling us to use it the dark without a flash giving away our own position to the enemy. Later, we were issued with the latest fully automatic weapon to use on our patrols.

During my time in Kenya, I was to spend nearly all of it on patrol. Our patrols consisted of five, allowing us to move faster and quieter through the dense bush. Each of us were armed to the teeth with our backpacks loaded with food supplies and ammunition. Overloading ourselves with supplies enabled us to remain on patrols for longer periods, thus avoiding having to return frequently to HQs to resupply. The weight of our backpacks felt as heavy as a sack of potatoes. The areas we patrolled were extensive, difficult, dangerous, and very hot; Kenya being on the Equator. At night we made camp using our groundsheets for cover and taking turns to stand guard.

Kenya is a beautiful country, rich in resources and wildlife. I had a Concertina camera that I always took with me on patrols to take photographs to show the family back home. I didn't mind taking risks to get a good picture. On one patrol we saw a herd of elephants strolling majestically and sedately through a gully. I decided to get closer for a better snapshot. Moving well away I quietly circled the herd when, unbeknownst to me, the bull elephant cut me off from its herd.

I would have put a blue bottomed monkey to shame as I zigged zagged over rocks, jumping and ducking through the bush to safety. My mates had a good laugh over that one. There was another time I had to run as fast. It was when I had a very bad dose of dysentery.

The latrine pits were about 200 yards outside army headquarters. I ran so fast I would have put the fastest world sprinter to shame. But I still didn't make it!

Whenever possible we chose high ground to pitch camp. Heights enabled us to view the landscape and spot any Mau Mau gangs on the move. On one of our patrols, I decided to move a short distance further down from camp to have a smoke, and at the same time look at the landscape from another angle. One of the most stringent rules of the army is to never let go of your rifle. This was such a fundamental order that even if you fainted whilst standing on parade, you were expected to still cling to your rifle when you hit the ground. When on active service going anywhere without your firearm was a serious and chargeable offence.

As I sat smoking, with my rifle across my knees well out of sight of my camp, I detected a movement to my left that instantly alerted me. About 50 feet away a large black panther was quietly watching me. It had been stalking me. Someone had once told me that if a panther leaps from a tree onto your back you are finished. I quickly sent off two successive shots that sent the animal scurrying back into the bush. In later years I wondered whether this black creature was indeed a panther, or was it a black leopard, or a black jaguar. I did some research and discovered that if it was an African panther then I had just experienced a close encounter with an extremely rare and elusive creature that few people ever see. As far as I'm aware, they have been found only in Laikipia County, Kenya. I was considered a crack shot with a rifle in basic training, earning high points in our shooting competitions but I'm thankful that on that occasion I missed hitting that magnificent animal.

On one of our patrols, we came across a deserted homestead which had its walls peppered with Mau Mau arrows. We knew nothing about the fate of its former white inhabitants. On this occasion I was with our platoon of about twenty men. We made camp whilst one of our men took it into his head to hunt for a gazelle that would give us fresh meat. He was a good distance from our camp when he saw a gazelle running in the distance.

He set his rifle sights on the running gazelle and pulled the trigger. It just so happened that when he fired off the shot our camp was in the background. I heard the shot and felt as if a red-hot iron had touched my arm. The round had grazed my arm. The shooter missed the gazelle, and we missed the taste of sweet meat that night. As for the shooter, he got the taste of army discipline by being put on half a dozen charges.

On our patrols we often passed through African villages where we were always eyed with suspicion by its inhabitants. They would often remain in their huts when they saw us coming. Orders had already come through that we were to kill all the dogs because of the spread of rabies. Every village had their scrawny, skinny, flea ridden dogs that you wouldn't want to find sleeping as a pet on the end of your bed.

There were five of us as we passed through one of these villages and the dogs came to sniff us out. I happened to be armed with a Sten gun which were used by commandos during the 2nd World War. They are light, small, and able to give off short bursts of rapid-fire. One of the dogs came forward and sat at my feet looking up at me. It was less than an arm's length away when I took aim and gave it a short burst of fire from the Sten I had. Puffs of dirt all around the dog showed up where the rounds landed. The dog didn't move but just kept looking up at me. It must have finally cottoned on to what I was about to do. It upped and took off as if it had a rocket up its rear. I was able to finish it off with my rifle and the faulty Sten was returned to HQ with a note about its condition.

One of the most dangerous creatures we faced in Kenya was the buffalo with its wide horn span that can reach up to 130cm and charge you at high speed without any provocation. We had to shoot one or two when they looked at us with their beady eyes weighing up whether to charge us or not. Rhinos were another little pest in Kenya we had to watch out for. One black night as the five of us camped, we felt the ground shake, and that brought us quickly to our feet. Something very big was sniffing us out. We all remained on guard that night, rifles cocked, ready, waiting for whatever it was to return. The next morning revealed the prints of a very large rhino.

There was a well-known Mau Mau leader who was nick-named 'Clubfoot.' Why he was called 'Clubfoot' I don't know; perhaps because he did have a club foot! He was an elusive character, who easily avoided our patrols. Intelligence reports reached us and informed us that he and his large gang were going to raid a farmhouse on a particular night.

Company C, to which I was attached, was immediately sent to the farm to set up an ambush. As darkness fell, we were ordered to take up our assigned ambush positions to give old 'Club foot,' and his gang a very warm welcome. By the time we were all in our positions it was pitch black. What followed was a typical British Army 'stuff up'. Lying low and silent in our ordered positions with our fingers on the triggers of our weapons we silently waited. Yes, we waited. And we waited. And we waited until the dawn slowly dawned, and the sun began to shine brightly down upon our heads. Surprise! Surprise! As we looked around, we were surrounded by our own men. Behind us were the trigger-happy Bren gunners with their guns pointed directly on backs. Directly in front of us were more of our men with their weapons pointed at us. Totally surrounded by allies!

Old "club foot" and his gang didn't show up; they must have smelled a rat. Had he turned up there would have been a massacre. We would have begun firing away in all directions without knowing that we were mowing down our own men. Whoever the high-ranking genius was that conjured up his master plan for this ambush was a complete fool. *By the* way *Club Foot, thanks for not turning up.*

Then there was the night when one of our guards panicked. I was with my C Company along with about twenty men camping out in an old farmhouse. I had finished my guard duty and was asleep when I was awakened by the shouting of my name. Apparently one of the guards thought we were under attack by a gang of Mau Mau and began firing his automatic in all directions. That was followed by even more rapid-fire taking place elsewhere. My mates thought I was lying dead. I looked at the place where I had been sleeping, and the wall inches above where my head had rested was riddled with bullet holes. To be killed accidently by your own side is known as death by 'friendly fire.' Oh! It is so very comforting to know that!

The Mau Mau would try to avoid our patrols rather than openly confront us. They knew they were no match against our weapons. We would set ambushes and quietly wait for any careless Mau Mau to walk into them. On one occasion four of them did. What followed is best forgotten. Looking back, it has caused one or two sleepless nights, but I do not try to dwell on it because I was under orders, doing my duty. God knows and God forgives.

In 1956 I was demobbed, having served my two years of National Service. I was awarded an African Service Medal and, along with my three mates, we left the army wondering how we would settle back into the humdrum of civilian life.

Civilian Life

I returned to my job as a groundsman in Bristol, being warmly welcomed back by my old friends but I was unable to settle back into the monotonous routine of civilian life; I was having serious thoughts about returning to Kenya. There was nothing to hold me in England; I was twenty, not married, and as free as a bird so, I could spread my wings and fly wherever I wished to go in this wide and wonderful world. On a whim, I decided back to Kenya, but this time, not by plane, not by ship but on a bicycle. I wanted it to be more interesting and see more of the world.

1956-1961 Age 20

News about my venture was somehow picked up by the media and appeared in the local newspaper. The BBC invited me to give an on-air interview after which I received a letter from someone who wanted to join me on my adventure, but I preferred to go it alone. There was a lot of planning I had to do. I bought myself a sturdy bike, got my British passport, purchased maps of the places I would have to cycle through, applied for the visas and documents and a host of other things that needed to be done before I left England. Finally, the day arrived when I set off on my bike one bright morning for Dover to catch the ferry across the Channel to France.

I had arranged to stop off at All-Saints Church in Basingstoke. The Vicar was the father of Lieutenant Brian Rudgard, with whom I served in Kenya. Brian and I were always on the same patrols together. I watched his back, and he watched mine. Despite the difference in rank, we became firm friends. For years I have sought to track him down without success. That night in the vicarage I enjoyed a good hearty dinner along with several fine sherries that his hospitable parents served up.

My first night in France was spent under a roadside bush trying to protect myself from a torrential downpour. The locals in the towns and villages that I passed through were all very friendly, and I did enjoy drinking their 'red stuff' renowned, they said, as the best in the world. I enjoyed the countryside and the freedom of being alone without a care in the world. I knew where I was heading with no set timetable to get there. I simply wanted to enjoy the ride.

I think it was about a week into France when I saw dark clouds ahead, indicating I was in for another soaking. I was in open country and the only option I had was to bed down in a ploughed field and cover myself with my groundsheet. I slept like a log. When I awoke the following morning, I saw boots all around me. They belonged to French labour workers who were hoeing the potato patch in which I had slept. They had left me alone not wishing to disturb my rest.

With lots of laughs and a hearty "au revoir" they waved me off as I mounted my bike and continued my journey.

Not far from the Spanish border I had a change of plan; I decided I would hitch-hike the rest of my journey to Kenya. I wanted to meet and talk to more people, but first I needed to get rid of the bike. I stopped at a small village where I met a group of locals, a couple of whom spoke broken English, and acted as my interpreter. The bargaining began. I think there were more glasses of wine passing across the table to me than there were French francs. In the end, they were happy to have the bike, I was happy to have the francs, and we were all happy to drink the wine together.

One motorist with whom I hitched a ride could only go so far and had to drop me off high in the Pyrenees between France and Spain. It was a clear, cold night as I lay in my sleeping bag under a pristine sky full of stars. I was at such a high elevation that the stars were like a canopy above and around me. It was an awe-inspiring sight with some fleeting thoughts about the existence of God passing through my mind.

I spoke neither French nor Spanish which made my trip more interesting and hilarious. I quickly learned I could get through by using the well-known universal language of mime and mimicry. It never let me down once. Moo like a cow for a meat sandwich, cluck like a chicken for a chicken meal, snort like a pig if your fancy is bacon, and if you like horsemeat, a delicacy in France, neigh like a horse. And lamb? Well, we all know what sheep sound like. If you wanted to buy cigarettes, you went through the motions of smoking one. When you entered a store, you pointed to what you wanted and gave the storekeeper the thumbs up with a big grin until he cottoned on and got it for you. It was an engaging way to meet new people and, mark my words, with this technique you'll never go hungry.

Hitch-hiking through Europe in the 50's was easier and much safer than it is today. Neither was it against the law. I hitched a lift to Barcelona where I was dropped off on the northern outskirts of this large city. I decided to walk from the Northern to the Southern end just to see more of it. With my knapsack on my back, and not a care in the world, I set off on my hike through this beautiful and ancient city with no notion at the time that 35 years later I would be returning to Barcelona on a special mission.

In the 1950's Spain was under the dictatorship of Franco. His Guardia Civil, (police) were everywhere and easily recognizable by their three-cornered hat known as the tricorn. They gave me the once over as I passed but fortunately, they never stopped or questioned me. Along the way I stayed in small taverns or cheap hotels where I had to sign a register and hand over my passport, and I recall leaving a note at one tavern next to my signature, "Kenya or Bust". Somewhere in that vast city there is an old hotel register with my name and message in it. I still wonder if those who read it after ever questioned if I made it?

I hitched a ride with a German couple to Granada who invited me to join them to see a bull fight. It was bloody spectacle. I shared in drinking from the wine skin holder that was passed between us. Along with the thousands of spectators I cheered the matador for his courage. When a bull refused to enter the ring to fight, white bandannas were waved from the hands of the thousands of spectators indicating the bull was a coward. Later, when I thought about the bulls that had chickened out, I thought they were the smart ones. Their motto must have been, 'better a live coward, than a dead bull'. When public opinion against bull fighting became more widespread in Spain it was rumoured that the bulls themselves were first in line to sign the petitions in favour of the bill!

From Granada I hitched to Gibraltar, a lump of rock captured by the British in 1704 and occupied by them ever since. Gibraltar's border officials were a bit reluctant to allow me to cross into their territory because I didn't look like someone who could add anything to the rock's economy. They were 100% right on that score. But they could not refuse me when they saw my British passport. The truth be known, I had spent over my budget in living the high life in France and Spain, and I was getting very low on my francs, pesos and pounds. On Gibraltar there was a mission to seafarers, a hostel for seafarers who fell on tough times. Although I was not Navy, I was warmly welcomed as an ex-army British serviceman who had served his country.

During my time on the Rock, I shared laughs and drinks with British servicemen. I climbed to its summit enabling me to look down 1,400-feet to the small airport below. The sight of Gibraltar's apes was an eye-opener. According to legend, Gibraltar would cease to belong to Britain if the apes ever left the rock. Winston Churchill seemed to have believed the legend, and repopulated Gibraltar with apes during 2nd World War.

If the apes ever ganged up for a pow-wow, and decided to leave the rock for greener pastures, the Brits would have to kiss the rock goodbye. Monkeys are sovereign and still rule the rock. Underground at Gibraltar, there are about 34 miles of tunnels, and during the WWII there was a secret plan to seal some British commandos inside in case there was any chance of losing Gibraltar to the Germans. From inside, they could keep a look-out on German warships crossing the Strait.

Before leaving Britain, I had planned to cross the fourteen miles Strait of Gibraltar to Morocco, North Africa, on a trawler or a cargo ship. However, France had now become involved in a war with Moroccan independent fighters who wanted to end France's rule in their land. Morocco became a warzone that put an end to me continuing my trip to Kenya. I had well and truly overspent on my budget which left me no alternative but to hitch-hike back through Spain and France. My destination, the British Embassy in Paris.

Before crossing Spain's border back into France, I was standing before the window of a small tienda (shop) displaying its goods. I had some loose change in my pocket and my eyes focussed upon just two things: a loaf of bread, and a cheap packet of cigarettes. The bread looked good, the cigarettes looked better. I was craving for a smoke. I chose a blue packet of ten with a picture of a camel as the manufacturer's logo. I lit up and deeply inhaled. The smoke smelt like camel's dung, the tobacco looked like camel's dung, and to be honest, it tasted like camel's dung. It satisfied my craving at the time, and it was the first of its kind I had ever smoked - and the last.

Hiking through France, an English motorist picked me up and dropped me outside the British Embassy in Paris. Arrangements were quickly made, I surrendered my passport in exchange for travel documents, and before long, I was on the ferry back to England to the place where my adventure first began.

Back In Bristol

Back in Bristol I got a job at an engineering company that made engine parts. Like many men my age, I turned to motor-bikes. My first was a 125cc Vespa bike which I considered to be much too slow. My second, a 250cc Enfield bike. Still too slow. My third, a 500cc BSA bike. A little better but still too slow. I had a need for speed! Finally, I settled with a 650cc Tiger 110. This Triumph bike, with a crash bar and two powerful spotlights attached was my pride and joy. It could do a "ton," i.e. 100 miles an hour.

With an old army friend who owned a powerful Matchless bike, we roared around towns and through small villages at full throttle with as much noise as our bikes could muster. We were not very popular with the locals, especially with mothers who tried to get their babies back to sleep in the wee hours of the morning.

To say that we were dare-devils is to put it mildly. Sometimes we would pick a straight stretch of road and take turns to see who could reach a ton, and back in the 50's that was quite a speed. Before he took his turn and I took mine we would hand over our watches to each other. If he crashed, I would have his watch as a token of our friendship. If I crashed, he would have my watch to remember me. They were crazy times, and I was living on the edge and loving it.

There are three separate incidents concerning my motor-bike days I still remember to this day. The first when I was referred to as a 'mad dog'. The second, when I was referred to as a 'pregnant camel', and third, when someone prayed for me.

The first incident occurred one afternoon when my shift work had finished. Hundreds of workers were lined up on the opposite side of the road facing the main gates of our engineering factory. They were patiently waiting for their red double-decker buses to take them home. This, I thought, was my time to impress them all. With a mighty roar and full throttle, I came tearing out of the main gates only to skid and spin on top of a man-hole-cover, I that sent me flying. Lifting myself up I heard roars of laughter coming from the other side of the road. The next morning one of my work mates said, "Peter, you came flying out of those gates like a mad dog".

The second incident involved the police. I was riding around Bristol and noticed heads were turning and watched me as I roared past; I was the centre of attention. Wow! It felt good. What I failed to hear was the siren of the Wolseley Police Car chasing me up the hill. As they slowly passed alongside, they waved me down. "Well," said the police officer, "that was some ride. You come up that hill weaving from side to side like a pregnant camel". They ticked me off, and I heard no more about the incident. I can't imagine one would get such a reasonable response today!

The third incident was when I stopped at an Open-Air Gospel meeting. As I watched and listened, allowing the engine to quietly tick over, one of its members approached me and asked, "young man where will you go when you die?" I was cocky in my reply, and answered, "I'm going straight to hell where a shovel is waiting for me to help shift the coal". He came close, looked me straight in the face and said very heatedly "no you won't. I'm going to pray for you, and I'll see you in heaven". Without another word he turned his back and walked away. Little did I know that his prayer would be answered eleven years later while I was sixteen thousand kilometres away, on the other side of the world.

Back in the 40's-50's immigrants from all over Europe were leaving in droves for Canada, Australia, New Zealand and Rhodesia (now Zimbabwe) in search of a new life. I was drawn to Rhodesia and had passed all medical and other requirements to set me on my merry way but for some reason that I still cannot remember, I had a change of mind and decided on Australia. So, I joined the ranks of becoming a 'Ten Pound Pom' immigrant. The year was 1961 and I was sped on my way "Down Under' on a 707 Qantas Airline on which wine, spirits and beer were freely served, and smoking permitted.

Australia & New Zealand

1962- 1964 Age 23-24

Kangaroo Point, Brisbane was the camp for incoming migrants. Jobs in Australia were plentiful, and I soon landed one as a salesman for Joseph Lucas Electrical. With a steady job, and what looked like a bright future, I settled into the Australian carefree way of life doing the routine of going to RSL Clubs, hotels and beer gardens with like-minded mates.

I remember Cloud Land, the iconic dancing hall where I kicked up my heels. I never considered myself a Fred Astaire or a Gene Kelly, but I did enjoy dancing. I liked the old fashion dance routines like the Waltzes, the Quick Step and the Fox Trots. The 50s and 60s was also the age of Rock and Roll, and I did some of that too.

There was an incident that occurred in one RSL Club that I deeply regret even to this very day. It had to do with the standing up for the British national anthem, "God Save the Queen", and I did not stand because I was too drunk to do so. An official came and reprimanded me, but instead of standing, I made some sort of derogatory remark about the Queen. He must have thought I was Irish Republican. Even though my mates came to my defence saying, "he's had one too many for the road", the official would not have a bar of it and I was quickly 'man-handled' out of the club.

I had an old friend in Liverpool that I used to knock around with before I left England and we had kept in touch over the years. He found out that I was in Australia and contacted me, wanting to know if I could catch up with him again in New Zealand. He already had a job at a hospital in Papatoetoe, a suburb in Auckland. After more than two years in Australia I felt the itch to venture out again into the unknown.

I must be honest here and explain that, for the next part of my life, my memory is a fuzzy mist. Facts are hazy, memories are incomplete and it reflects the state of my mind that I cannot remember when, or with whom I booked my flight to New Zealand. There are things I do remember, for example, there were several farewell booze parties with friends before I left. I remember waving to people at the top of the steps before entering the aircraft. I remember enjoying drinks on the flight over, and I remember an air hostess telling me "I think you've had enough to drink" when I asked for another. This portion of my life was filled with too much drink and a sorrowful lack of genuine priorities.

Upon disembarking in New Zealand, I asked an airport official how I could get to Papatoetoe where my friend worked. "Never heard of it", he replied. I told him it was a place somewhere in Auckland. "Auckland! Auckland", he cried' "Don't you know where you are? You're in Christchurch on the South Island!". I thought I must have been really sozzled when I booked my air ticket not to have given my destination as Auckland. I'm not even sure how I got from Christchurch over to the North Island. I must have used what little money I had to pay for the ferry from the South to the North Island. I can't remember, it's mostly blank.

I remember hitch-hiking through the North Island and vaguely remember a Salvation Army Hostel where I was given a meal, a shower and a bed. I recall sleeping on a bench in a small railway station and eating a meal in a café that I knew I could not pay for. Now, since I was not beaten up by the Mauri owner, I'm assuming they took a good, long look at me and decided they felt more compassion for my state than anger for my non-payment. I left the café and encountered a red telephone booth in which I propped myself up to rest my tired body. I also remember not having any cigarettes to satisfy my craving for a smoke. I was a hobo, a vagrant, stony broke, homeless, and down on my luck but I thought that when I caught up with my friend in Papatoetoe, all would be well. That meeting, however, was never to take place.

I had a dream or was it a vision? I still don't know. *I saw myself sitting on a low rock wall watching the traffic passing by. I saw myself completely relaxed. I saw a black car. It was coming toward me, and I knew it was going to stop to pick me up.* To this day I cannot explain how this came about. I have no answer. As I continued walking, I made no effort to thumb a lift. Then I recognized ahead that low wall I had seen myself sitting upon. I sat upon it and waited as streams of cars continued to pass by, but I made no effort to flag any of them down. Then in the distance I saw a black car coming toward me. That was the one I saw in my vision. I waited until it was near and casually got up and flagged it down. It stopped and I climbed into the back seat. I cannot remember anything about the driver and during the journey there was just silence. I was deposited at the bottom of Queens Street, Auckland.

I didn't know what day of the week it was, or in what direction I was supposed to go to get to Papatoetoe where my friend worked. I craved for a smoke and began to walk up Queen Street with my eyes glued to the gutter hoping to find cigarette butts that smokers toss away. As I neared the top of Queen Street a man approached me and invited me to come to church. Apparently, it was a Sunday. I was about to turn him down but changed my mind thinking someone in his church might be a smoker. So, I followed him inside, sitting with him at the back of a crowded Baptist Tabernacle Church. Behind the pulpit from which the Reverend was speaking was a large church organ with its many pipes that looked like a row of cigarettes.

The man who fished me off the street was Peter Plummer, the leader of the young adult's fellowship. He and his family invited me to their home and took care of my immediate needs and that was the beginning of a life-long friendship that I feel deeply to this very day.

Peter Plummer
1934-1994

THE FISHERMAN'

He did not know the catch he'd make.
The place? The man? The when?
He knew he was Christ's fisherman
A fisherman of men.

It was so long ago he fished
the streets of Auckland City.
Intent to win the lost for Christ,
to seek and offer pity.

The man he caught was down on luck,
his eyes glued to the gutter.
A vagrant looking for a butt,
that might hold some tobacca.

Come, he said, please come to church
so, he went along to listen
As he heard the preacher speak
His eyes began to glisten.

The man he caught that Sunday night
turned out as quite a catch
He felt the love of Jesus Christ
no love on earth could match.

That homeless vagrant became Christ's man,
When Jesus called him Mine,
He preached the Gospel o'er fifty years,
since that fisherman cast his line.

I was the man the fisherman caught,
and he became my brother.
That fisherman has passed to his reward;
His name was Peter Plummer.

I began to realise that my life was in a mess. I was an addict. A captive held bound by addictions from which I could see no escape. Under the powerful preaching of the Rev. Fred Carter, I knew that God was calling me, and I responded to His call. An overwhelming sense of God's peace and presence flooded through my whole being at that time; I felt I was living outside of my own body in the very presence of God Himself. I was baptized before a large congregation, publicly acknowledging my faith in Jesus Christ. From that moment I knew I was a captive of Jesus Christ. My life had been changed forever.

Reflecting over my past I can see how God's protective hand was over me from the moment of my birth. I was born a nobody with no real family or identity, but God saw me differently. In His eyes I *was* a somebody, whom He loved and would take and change for His own glory.

My thoughts went back eleven years to when I approached an Open-Air Gospel meeting in Bristol on my motorbike. I remembered my cocky reply to the fellow's question "where will you go when you die?", I also remembered how he heatedly replied, "no you won't. I'm going to pray for you, and I'll see you in heaven". I believe that one day when my time in this realm is done, and I enter heaven, I will hear that good man say, "I told you so."

From this point my life took a 180-degree turnabout. I became an active member of the Baptist Tabernacle and part of the Young Adults Group involved in its outreach program. Under the leadership of Peter, we went 'street fishing' that entailed inviting people to church. We also went to Auckland's docks where we were able to board ships and talked to merchant seamen about Christ. Something that is almost impossible to do today.

I landed a job with Joseph Lucas Company whose products I was already familiar with having worked for them in Australia. The thought of drinking alcohol never entered my mind, I was, however, still very much addicted to smoking. I remember walking to Church one Sunday morning with my Bible in one hand and a cigarette in the other merrily puffing away. It dawned on me suddenly that I had to kick the habit. And so, the battle began, and what a battle it turned out to be! I would buy a packet of twenty cigarettes, smoke one, feel guilty, and toss the rest of the pack away. It was costing me a fortune to buy cigarettes just to dump half of them. I persisted, and fought myself, and eventually, I did kick the habit.

The firm I worked for in Auckland transferred me to Wellington to cover the Upper and Lower Hutt districts as their salesman. I became part of the OAC (Open Air Campaigners) team led by a man named Noel Gibson, well known for his open-air preaching. Every Saturday night we preached on the streets in the centre of Wellington where I would share my own testimony in how I found peace with God through Christ.

Tasmania, Missionary Training College

It was 1963 and I was beginning to feel a call to full-time service. I began to think about foreign missionary work. There was a WEC Missionary Training College in Tasmania to whom I had already applied for training. I was accepted. WEC (Worldwide Evangelisation for Christ) was a missionary society started by a well-known English cricketer named C.T. Studd who once played for England. He spent his life in dedicated service to the Lord, serving in China, India, and Africa. In 1913 he formed the World Evangelisation Crusade (whose name later changed and is now known as WEC International) which still operates to this day.

In one of my quiet times with the Lord I learned a truth that was to hold me steadfast throughout my entire Christian life. I was often bombarded with questions from well-meaning Christians asking if I spoke in tongues. They would ask me; "have you received the baptism of the Holy Spirit?" They referred to it as the Second Blessing. Even though I was young in the faith I felt uncomfortable about their belief.

I was reading Paul's letter to the Colossians 2:9 that said, *"For in Christ all the fullness of Deity lives in bodily form, and you have been given fullness in Christ, who is the head over every power and authority"*. The truth of these words seemed to leap off the page into my heart and mind. I Instantly understood I had received the fullness of Christ at second birth. (John 3:1-8). My usefulness to Him would depend solely upon my abiding in spiritual union with Him. (John 15:4). Without Him I knew I could do nothing. It was not more of His life that *I* needed. I already had His fullness when I was born again. It was more of my life that *He* needed.

My two years at the Missionary Training College was an enriching experience. Under the leadership of Stuart Dinnen, I began to grow in my understanding of the Bible as the infallible Word of God. His messages were always centred on the deeper things of Christ and of the importance of maintaining a life of meditation and prayer.

While at this college, I attended the Launceston Central Baptist Church where I taught Sunday School. Listening to the pastor's messages each Sunday I learned much about public speaking. He was a good orator; his messages were crafted in such an orderly way they were easy to remember and difficult to forget.

The program at WEC College was thoroughly Bible based. There was no mention of any European or American 19th or 20th century theologians who flatly denied the basic doctrines of the Christian faith. Thirty years later I had to study these theologians at a Baptist Theological College to graduate for my diploma as a Baptist pastor. Wading through their theological theories was akin to swimming through thick sand. As Spurgeon said, *'it all amounts to nothing more than hot air, wind and wastepaper'*. As my studies at the WEC College was coming to an end, I began to think ahead as to what part of the world the Lord would have me serve Him. My thoughts slowly began to focus on South America, specifically Colombia.

I returned to New Zealand from Tasmania to complete a graduate's course before leaving for the foreign field. The leader was Ivor Davies. He was an ex-missionary who served in the Congo in 1913. Ivor Davies was one of the godliest men I have ever had the privilege of meeting; I can still remember his rich, Welsh voice soaring high above the congregations when we were singing "Guide Me O Thou Great Jehovah" in our packed Baptist Tabernacle.

WEC Headquarters was situated in Mt. Eden, a suburb of Auckland. I would ascend the slopes of Mt. Eden to be alone with Lord on many evenings. They were precious times, but finally, my time had come for me to leave my mountain top retreat and venture down into the valley to do the work God had called me to do. I was about to leave for Colombia, South America as I had already enrolled in the Edinburg Language School, close to the Mexican border in Texas, USA. Just prior to leaving, Ivor Davies laid his hands upon my head and prayed. I felt the warmth of God's love and power flow through me and in that same instance I knew I had received the gift of teaching. The following day, with just one suitcase, I boarded the ship for Miami. USA.

America & Colombia

I arrived in Miami on 25/8/1967 according to my old passport, which I still have. The first challenge I faced was understanding the language in Miami. It was a mixture of Spanish and the southern American drawl. I couldn't understand a word of what was being said over the loudspeakers advising ongoing travellers what buses to catch and where to catch them. It all sounded double Dutch to me. Eventually a helping hand directed me to the Greyhound bus that would take me the 1,797 miles, and cross 3 times zones to the Edinburg Bible College, in Texas. It was quite a trip, and I met and talked with some very interesting characters along the way. By the time I arrived my rear end was so sore from sitting on the rocks that the Greyhound bus service referred to as "seats".

The Edinburg Bible College was established to train Mexican students for the Christian ministry and used as a Spanish language school for missionaries going to South America. I was allocated a caravan on campus, and arrangements were made for me to have my meals with the students in the main dining hall. Frijoles, frijoles, and more frijoles at every meal (beans). I was thrown into the deep end as far as having to learn Spanish as there were times I had to talk in front of the students in Spanish who would spend much of the lesson correcting my mistakes. They were hilarious times, and we would all double up with laughter over some of my gaffes.

I remember two major events that took place when I was in the USA. In 1967 Hurricane Beulah came over with a devastating force that caused our camp to be evacuated. And, in 1968 the assassination of John F. Kennedy. They were difficult times for Americans whom I found to be some of the most generous people I had ever encountered. I remember one day when a group of us were sitting and chatting together, one of them pulled out a revolver. Now, I knew that Americans were permitted to carry firearms, but I was surprised to see this young fellow who was preparing to go the south as a missionary feeling that he needed it to defend his family and himself. I wondered what kind of missionary he would make with his Bible in one hand and his gun in the other.

The next passport stamp denotes my arrival at Bogota's International Airport, on 20/6/1968. Colombia, known as the "Gateway to South America," had gained its independence from Spain in 1819, under the leadership of Simón Bolívar. In every government building you will find a mural of Bolívar sitting on a white charger, proclaiming his victories over Spain.

Pat Symes, an Australian, was the Field Leader, who went to Colombia in the 1930's. The growing Evangelical churches at that time were under severe persecution by guerrilla groups who threatened and murdered the church leaders who denounced corruption, defended human rights, and opposed the drug cartels. Pat risked his life in going to Colombia during that period. He was a man I came to admire in every way. A quiet man, a good listener, and one endowed with wisdom revealing he had a very close walk with the Lord. He asked if I would go to a town called Ibagué, southeast of Bogotá, where a small group of evangelical Christians resided.

I spent my first night in an enclosure that housed the poorest of the poor. I slept on a camp-bed and there was absolutely no privacy for myself, or the residents. I could hear the snoring, coughing, and talking of those around me. In the centre of the enclosure was a large trough that was used to act as the water supply for the residents. It didn't worry me; I was used to roughing it, but it did worry the small band of Christians when they saw how I was living so they found a room near their house church for me to rent. No one in the Church spoke English so my Spanish rapidly began to improve.

The congregation had little of this world's possessions, but what they did have was of far more value than anything this world could ever offer. Oh, what a vibrant faith and love for Jesus they expressed as we met together in our meetings of Bible study and praise. I was literally lost in wonder and spiritual ecstasy before the Lord.

Among the congregation was a cobbler who volunteered to cook me a meal every day. He, his wife and four children lived in a small hut on the edge of Ibagué. I had no means of preparing food for myself and neither was there any fast-food shops within walking distance from where I lodged so I had to accept his offer. The family was very poor. I still remember their menu. It never changed; a watery potato soup with a little meat and an egg thrown in. The warmth and love of this humble family made that food taste like manna from heaven.

I had to take the funeral for one of our church members neighbours. Before the burial there is a ceremony called the Wake. The deceased person is laid out in an open casket or on a table for family members and friends to pay their last respects before burial. In this case the deceased was stretched out on top of the dinner table where a meal had been prepared for me to eat. The deceased was well dressed in a suit and looked to all the world as if he was just having a snooze. I couldn't help seeing the funny side of it as I began to eat with a dead man as my table companion, and no, I did not ask him to please pass me the pepper and salt.

I was asked to go to a nearby village to visit a young girl of about 11 years of age who was gravely ill. The home was crowded with her family, friends, and neighbours and before I prayed for the girl's healing, I boldly announced to the large crowd of onlookers that God was going to heal this child from her sickness. I prayed most fervently for her healing and earnestly wanted to see her restored to full health and strength, but early the next morning I was informed the girl had died.

As I lead her casket along the dirt road to the cemetery, followed by her family and friends, and watched by the crowds who turned up for the funeral, I felt all eyes upon me. What were they thinking? What was I thinking? I felt humiliated and ashamed. Why? Why? Was the main question going through my mind. Why had not God healed her? Then I began to realize I had presumed that God *would* heal her. I was guilty of committing the sin of presumption. The Psalmist wrote, "*Keep back your servant also from presumptuous sins; let them not have dominion over me; then shall I be upright, and shall be innocent from any great transgression*" Psalm 19:13. As one hymn writer puts it;

"Thy righteous judgments whilst we see
On sloth and on simplicity
And whilst presumption's fate we trace
Preserve us, Jesus, by Thy grace."

Unknown hymn writer

Throughout my long Christian ministry, I have been very careful never to take God for granted again, and I have avoided committing the sin of presumption.

I spent two years in Ibagué before Pat Symes called me back to Bogotá to pastor a growing city church. I was leaving behind a vibrant house church of Christian friends whom I came to love and who had so enriched my own life. I would dearly miss them.

Back in Bogotá, I became acquainted with another missionary named Colin Crawford. Colin was an outstanding preacher with his own radio broadcast. He had a very effective ministry that went far beyond the borders of Colombia. I also met a Peace Co-Worker called Dave Cave, a committed Christian, and his wife, Liz, who were a source of encouragement to me in my work. Colin, Dave, and I became firm friends encouraging each in the work of the Lord. Colin passed to his reward a few years ago, and I still maintain contact with Dave and Liz who now live in the UK.

The church in Bogotá had a larger congregation than the one in Ibagué. I was warmly welcomed and quickly settled into the ministry of teaching God's word. I remember the occasion when one of our poorest members in our church was robbed. She lived in one room with just the bare necessities of life, and while attending church one Sunday morning a truck pulled up outside her place, broke open the door, and stole everything she had, including her bed. I can never forget what she said to me. '*Hermano Pedro*, '*me han robado.*' "Brother Peter, they have robbed me." Then she smiled, and added, "Jesus knows, and I can still praise His wonderful name." Our church was quick to help her, but I wondered just how many well-fed Christians back home would have said the same!

It was always a joy to see someone commit their life to Jesus and then follow through by being baptized. Come hail, snow, howling wind or freezing cold, nothing could stop these robust people from entering a freezing river to be baptized, and while they were standing in that freezing water, they would give their long testimonies on how they came to know the Lord. And I, standing waist deep next to them ready to baptize would gradually lose all feeling in my legs. Many-a-time I had to hold onto someone's arm to be helped out of a river.

As a single male in Colombia, I had to face my own personal challenges; I was often approached by females who made their intentions very clear. Foreigners were considered a good catch as marriage partners because of the possibility that they could enhance the social and financial status of some poor Colombian girl. I was fixed in my determination to remain pure in body and soul. I made it a policy I would never compromise myself by entering a house where a woman dwelt alone. Throughout my long ministry both at home and abroad I have kept to that policy, the only homes I would enter would be that of elderly retirees. I remembered what Paul wrote, "*there must not even be a hint of sexual immorality*" (Eph. 5:3).

Then there came a time when I went through what early Christians called 'The Dark Night of the Soul.' This was a time when I felt spiritually abandoned by God. I began to harbour doubts about the divinity of Jesus. I was asking myself many questions, such as, was Jesus really God incarnate? Here I was, in Colombia, seeking to bring the light of Christ to its people and yet having doubts about His Person. I felt darkness in my soul. This was not something I could just shake off. It was having an effect upon me, physically, emotionally, and spiritually. I prayed fervently to the Lord and felt prompted to read the Gospel of John. This I did in one sitting. During this reading, the Holy Spirit confirmed to my heart and mind that Jesus was both human and divine. I have never doubted the divinity of Jesus since, or what He said about Himself as true. I am now convinced that at that moment I was under the severe attack of the devil.

One of the most moving experiences I had in Colombia was my visit to an isolated leper colony called, 'Agua de Dios' (Water of God or Living Water of God). The Colony was like a small township where people with leprosy, and their families, lived together. In Biblical times leprosy was considered a curse from God as a profound impurity and Jewish law stated that lepers maintain at least twelve cubits (about sixteen feet) from the nonleprous. If a leper were to approach a Jew, the Jew would give him a wide berth but when a leper approached Jesus to be healed, Jesus did not shrink back in horror "lest He become infected. He breached this law of separation by touching the leper and healing him." (Mark 1:40-45). The belief that leprosy was a curse from God had long been rejected, along with maintaining any distance from the infected person.

Upon entering the leper colony, the inhabitants came crowding around us, Colin, Dave and myself, holding and touching our hands, arms, and face. They wanted to feel accepted and embraced by someone who cared. We held a church service, and the hall was packed. As I looked about, I saw signs of leprosy all around me. There was the loss of digits, skin nodules, facial disfigurement, and signs of amputation. Uninfected children were sitting on the laps of their parents or family being caressed by their infected parents. There was no separation. There existed that invisible bond of love that bound them all together. It took some time for me to pull myself away from these beautiful people. I continue to cherish the memories I have of them and shall do so until my dying day.

I was asked by Pat Symes to go high up into the Andes Mountains to where a Christian family lived, and where they had no ministry. To reach my destination I first had to travel a very long distance on a rickety old bus with its passengers of pigs, chickens, and goats, along with their owners, and the bus route ended at the base of the Andes. From there I was expected to go the rest of the way by horse, and two horsemen with a spare horse were waiting for me, but I'd never ridden a horse in my life! I still don't know how I got up onto that horse. Did they give me a leg-up like they would give a lady?

As we slowly ambled up the mountain slopes, I became aware of how isolated this place was, a man could disappear forever here although I had no fear that this would happen to me. I was always conscious of God's protection. After more than an hour or so we finally came to a small hamlet high in the Andes where a woman, her husband and their three young children lived. I was glad to get off that horse for my backside was surely sore. Years later, while swapping stories with my sister Freda, she told me how she felt when riding her first horse; after a lengthy period of bouncing up and down in the saddle she said she felt as though she had just come out of a hospital labour ward after giving birth to her firstborn!

I was given a meal after which I expected to have a Bible study with the family around the dinner table, but word had spread of my coming, and a meeting had already been arranged for that evening. As I was finishing my meal people began to arrive in their ones and twos into the house. Some had trekked over long distances to hear what this missionary had to say, and surprisingly quickly the place became crowded with more than 50 adults and children. I felt so humbled and at the same time deeply privileged to be able to share God's Word with these isolated, warm-hearted Christians. The Lord surely has His own people in some of the most isolated places on earth.

Bogotá is at an altitude of 2,640 meters (8,660 feet) above sea level and in winter it can become bitterly cold. One winter season I came down with a terrible cold and was admitted to our local medical clinic in Bogota. The doctors feared I had pneumonia as ugly cold sores appeared on my upper lip. They looked terrible and I felt embarrassed about meeting and talking to anyone. The doctors recommended a short stay in a warmer climate, so I left Bogotá and headed down from the mountains to the hotter climate on the lower plains known as the Llanos, where I could sweat the cold out of my system.

The Llanos is where the indigenous peoples of Colombia live. One of our missionaries, Wilf Watson, an old timer, was working among a tribe called the Guahibo. The indigenous tribes are looked down upon by some Colombians as an inferior race of people without a soul. I recall the incident when one of the Guahibos went to shake hands with a Colombian only to have his hand rudely pushed away. It was while I was with the friendly Guahibos that I got my first taste of that little armoured creature, the Armadillo. The Armadillo is a delicacy the Guahibo people relish but I can't say I found it yummy yum yum. It tasted something like chicken, but nothing like the 'finger lickin' Kentucky we have at home. It was my first, and last, taste of an Armadillo when I learned it could be the cause of leprosy!

When I returned to Bogotá, I asked the Colombian welfare authorities if I could visit prisons as a chaplain. I felt I could offer something to people whose lives had cast them into dark places. Permission was granted to me, and I was issued with a special Cedula (Identity Card) allowing me free access within prisons for this purpose. I contacted the British Embassy in Bogotá about what I had in mind, and they immediately offered their help; they let me borrow Embassy films, books, and other educational material that I could use on my visits. The prisoners, under the supervision of a guard, would gather and I would show an educational film on something of interest to them.

During the day, the prisoners were allowed out of their cells to wander freely around the courtyard, and this enabled me to have close contact by walking and talking with them about Christ and His love for them. My impression was that many of the inmates were political prisoners, rather than gang members or actual criminals as dictated by modern standards. I got to know the Jefe (chief) of the prison well and we had many chats together in his office. I think he always felt threatened in his position and would never let anyone know where he lived, he always struck me as someone who remained on his guard.

There lived on the outskirts of Bogotá an elderly Christian lady named Maria whose teenage children still lived with her. To get to her home I had to catch a tram to the end of the line and then walk quite a distance across a muddy paddock towards her small home and my only guide on dark nights was the light shining in the distance from her small house. Dogs were a real threat as I crossed over that dark empty paddock, they were not kept as pets, but as guard dogs trained to protect and to fight. I used to carry an umbrella and a child's toy cap gun to keep them at bay!

Maria was a widow. She had been a Christian for many years, and she lived in a poverty-stricken area called La Primavera. We started an evening Bible study in her home to which she invited her friends. Every week I made the trek across the paddock, in the dark, on the alert for aggressive dogs, to her home for a Bible study. Her neighbours that came along with their children were often soaked to the skin whenever they were caught in a downpour and I doubted that some would even have dry clothes to change back into when they returned to their homes.

There was an empty hall close by, and it was decided by the villagers that we should begin holding our Bible studies there, which meant that slowly our small numbers could increase. Since leaving Colombia I have learned that it is now one of the largest churches in Bogotá today and it all started with an elderly widow, named Maria. When I get to heaven, I'll have no problem finding Maria among the countless saints. I shall just look for one of heaven's brightest crowns and there she will be.

Prior to leaving Colombia I received an aerogramme from a Christian lady in New Zealand whose surname was 'Horrell.' She had seen my prayer card in a friend's home and wanted to meet this 'other Peter Horrell' serving the Lord in Colombia. She also had a son named Peter. They invited me to join them on holiday when I returned home on furlough, this is a type of sabbatical for ministers to have a break. It was to become a life-long friendship with the Horrell family in New Zealand.

New Zealand. Furlough. Marriage

It was time for furlough, so from Bogotá I caught a flight to Miami where I boarded a ship bound for New Zealand, as I had promised the Horrell's. As I disembarked at Auckland, about two weeks later, I heard someone call my name. Fred Carter, Ivor Davies, and an elder of my Church, Stan Conway, were there to welcome me home. The stamps on my passport (which I have kept all these years) show I had left New Zealand in August 1967 and returned in 1972; I had been away for 5 years.

I had not been thinking of marriage when I left Colombia for furlough; at that time being a single man in Colombia had been somewhat problematic and though I did want to return, I knew that doing so as a single man was not going to be ideal. So, I enrolled in the Bible College of New Zealand for a 1-year refresher course to give myself time to plan my next adventure.

During that year I met up with Caroline Cardinal, a lady with whom I had studied in Tasmania 10 years ago. Caroline had completed her training for missionary service, at the same time as me and she had been working from the Sydney headquarters of the same Mission that I had been serving with in Colombia. Her role entailed sending Bible correspondence courses to Asia and the Pacific Islands written in simple, concrete English to those with English as a second language. She had been working in a counselling role via the mail to some thousands of correspondents. Caroline had come to New Zealand to meet up with her sister Heather as they had planned an adventure holiday to South America together, but she never made the trip, due to reasons I will explain, although her sister and friend did complete the trip without her.

Caroline had found a job in a legal office in Auckland and had secured accommodation at a Youth Hostel which was part of a youth outreach from Auckland Baptist church. Ten years had passed without any correspondence with each other but somehow, our direction in life had been strangely parallel. I recognised her and invited her to a prayer group run by WEC Mission – with whom I had served in Colombia, and she had served in the Sydney headquarters. From her account, God clearly spoke to her at that prayer group telling her, "You are not going to South America with your sister, you are going there with Peter." She maintains to this day that it was a shock to the system as we had only just reconnected days earlier after 10 years of absence and no prior thoughts of each other. Needing confirmation and clarity she asked God for something more concrete to confirm that it was indeed God speaking to her. That came the next morning from her normal morning devotions in Ephesians 3:15 "But the God of peace shall be umpire in your heart, for to this peace He has called you together into one body. Now be thankful." It was her prayer answered and confirmation delivered that this was the path the Lord had planned for her.

As I was accompanying her home from the prayer group, I felt compelled to invite her to meet up with me again for a meal. She agreed and two days later we went out for dinner together. After the meal I took her to a mountain overlooking Auckland harbour and I began to realize that what God had said to her was also His answer to me! I proposed on that first date, knowing that this was God's intention for my life as well. The following day, I received a letter from a friend in the South Island of New Zealand saying that they believed God was giving me a wife, (they could not possibly have known what had just occurred in Auckland) and they had gifted me a cheque for $300 for that purpose which, 53 years ago, was a lot of money. That money became our rings as, 3 months later, Caroline became my wife. Although events happened fast, we found that our commitment produced love and, in our case, peace that we were moving in the direction chosen by God for us.

We were married at Caroline's home church in Bethel, Brisbane in 1973. Surrounded by her relatives and our close friends, our wedding was a joyous and blessed occasion. Peter Plummer, who 'fished' me off the streets of Auckland was my best man.

I had not seen my family for 14 years and so we decided to spend part of our honeymoon in the UK with my family in Okehampton. It was the policy of our Mission that newlyweds should not return to missionary service for twelve months after their marriage so during this period, we did deputation work around Australia instead.

America, Edinburg Language College

A year later we left for America so that Caroline could attend the same language college I had attended. Whilst in America we were asked by WEC HQ to divert from Colombia to Venezuela, where there were fewer missionaries, and this we did.

VENEZUELA

Our Venezuelan team leader was Allan King, and his wife Ann, who had served in Venezuela for many years. We settled into the small town of Acarigua, where a warm, vibrant Christian fellowship welcomed us, and that was to become our home for the next twelve months. However, as God had confirmed my ministry as teaching the Word of God, thus leading people to walk in a life of faith, it became obvious that we needed to be involved in a growing church. We were therefore sent by Allan to Barquisimeto where I conducted a nightly bible institute amongst the youth. In the beginning Caroline struggled to communicate in Spanish, but she received helped from a professor in linguistics, who was an ex-Jesuit priest and who belonged to the fellowship. It came to pass that Caroline's command of Spanish eventually far exceeded my own.

Having been told in America that we would not be able to have children of our own we began to think of adoption; a doctor friend in New Zealand knew of an orphaned infant and were preparing to help. Then came the good news for which the fellowship had been praying - Caroline was with child and when he was born we named him Peter-Andrew. Our congregation, being Spanish, were slightly disappointed that we did not name the baby Pedro-Andres. Later, Caroline become pregnant again but unfortunately, she lost the baby.

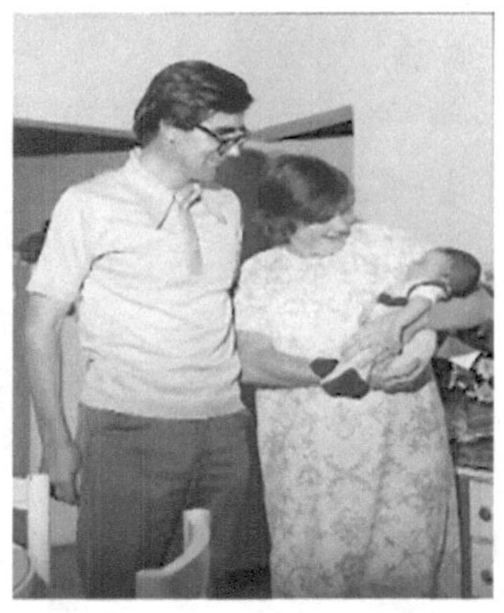

There was a member of the church who worked for a major Venezuelan newspaper who asked me to write weekly editorials about the evangelical Christian beliefs. This I happily accepted as I saw it as a chance to have a wider audience to share the Gospel of Christ. I wrote under the penname "Theophilus" (Acts 1:1). I chose the name because we had just saved a tortoise from being run over by a truck! We took it home for a pet and named it Theophilus (hence the penname) and our infant son Peter-Andrew used to sit on its back.

Pictures from Bible Seminar – Barquisimeto, Venezuela

Whilst in Barquisimeto, an American Mission asked if we could be seconded to them to develop a full time Bible Training Seminary in one of its evangelical churches. We agreed and commenced nightly Bible studies for young Christians who were interested in future ministry. I put together it's curriculum and acted as Dean while Caroline, a gifted musician, put together a music programme and taught music to the participants. It was a privilege to be able to teach young students who one day would become pastors in their own country.

We had now been away for four years and due for another furlough, so, with our 18 month-old toddler Peter-Andrew, we began the first leg of our journey to the UK where we hit a snag that prevented us going on to Australia. A new law had been passed whilst we were away that stopped anybody not holding an Australian passport re-entry into Australia. I had travelled to Venezuela on my British passport, having not yet applied for Australian citizenship. Our onward flight to Australia was already booked and due to leave within two days. I was in a pickle. We contacted the Australian Embassy who wouldn't help until Caroline told them her father, who had cancer, and was deteriorating, wanted to see his grandson before he died. The Embassy pulled out all stops and enabled us to catch our booked flight back to Australia. The Lord had answered our prayer. William Charles Cardinal passed away in September 1978 and was blessed with meeting and nursing his grandchild.

Australia, Baptist Theological College

For some time, I'd been thinking of a home ministry in Australia. I wanted to further my theological studies at the Baptist Theological College of Queensland. It would take me four years to complete but the College gave me a year's credit because of my previous service.

TOWNSVILLE, 1979

Meanwhile I was asked to stand in as interim Pastor at the Baptist Church in Townsville. Just prior to leaving for Townsville, our two-year-old was playing, and swinging on a concrete bird bath in a friend's garden. Unknown to us, the concrete basin was not securely connected to its stand, and it came down breaking his leg. With our son's leg in plaster, and our small car packed with our belongings, we headed north to Townsville. It was the cyclone season and north of Mackay the road was flooded but a businessman in the Townsville Church radioed one of his trucks which fellow helped us get to through the flood to Townsville. My interim Pastorship was for twelve months, and though I could have accepted a call to stay longer, I felt I had to attend college in person to get my Diploma of Theology. When I received a call from the Greenslopes Baptist Church, in Brisbane I accepted, enabling me to attend the colleges' daily lectures.

Greenslopes

Founded in 1920, Greenslopes had developed an all-age Sunday School that attracted over 200 young students. It has a fine evangelical history of being a Church with an emphasis on outreach. It was late evening when we first arrived and were inundated with about 20 young people who welcomed us. What an introduction! During my time there as Pastor I was to officiate some of these youngsters' weddings.

I began to follow the advice given to me by the Baptist Pastor thirty years earlier in Tasmania by writing out my messages in full. I did not know it at the time, but taking notes have proved to be a tremendous source of help when I began writing in my later years. Beside taking the morning and evening Sunday services, I was involved in leading the mid-week prayer meeting, the elders meeting, and maintaining the list of people who I should visit. On top of that I often had to burn the midnight oil to keep up with my theological studies.

There were incidents that occurred in Greenslopes that added spice to my life, and I thank the Lord for blessing me with a sense of humour; some would say a wicked sense of humour. I'll never forget the first baptism I took in the Greenslopes Church. How could I ever forget! There was a fisherman's rubber garment in the vestry that was used by previous Pastors when baptizing new converts. I didn't know if this was the way a baptism was normally conducted in this Church so, not wishing to be different, I put it on over my suit. It covered all my lower body reaching up to my chest.

Standing in the baptismal pool of a packed Church, up to my waist alongside a young convert, I began to pray the baptismal prayer. "I now baptise you in the Name of the Father, the Son and the Holy Spirit," and at the same time I plunged him deep beneath the water. In doing so, however, I bent over so far that water poured in over the top of the garment filling it up and I walked off with the sound of 'slosh, slosh, slosh' resounding through the Church like a theme tune, and to the sounds of laughter from the pews! I had a good old laugh about it too.

There was also in the vestry a black cloak that preachers used years ago when they stood in the pulpit to give their sermons. It was a heavy piece of black material that I had taken an interest in; it was well made and may have dated back to the 1920's. I wondered to myself whether I was expected to wear this on Sundays? "Do I or do I not? Should I or should I not?" I could imagine myself looking like Count Dracula wearing it as I stood in the pulpit. In the end I wasn't game to wear it because the thought of looking like the Count would have had me laughing too much to be able to preach the sermon.

I remember being asked to take the funeral of an unknown person at a crematorium and this was to be my first crematorium funeral. I was given instructions on what buttons I should use and what buttons I should avoid when I stood behind the Lectern. I was told, "press this one, but *don't* press that one. Don't press too hard or too long, otherwise ..." and was told the following story by a crematorium official.

A pastor was concluding his service ending with the solemn words *"dust thou art to dust returnest"* while at the same time pressing the button that automatically closed the curtain and sent the casket downward to the crematorium below. He ended the service with the benediction, and as the people rose to leave there were gasps of "what the ...?" Music was heard again; the curtains came apart again; and the casket came up again for all to see. The pastor must have touched a button that his twiddling fingers should not have touched. Oh! I was so glad I wasn't in the shoes of that pastor. A quick burial, and an even quicker resurrection! I couldn't help laughing.

We spent roughly 3 years in Greenslopes, and during that time Caroline gave birth to a beautiful blue-eyed little girl whom we named Tania, and when my daughter was almost 6 months old, we found out that Caroline had been blessed once again! Our third and final child was born a boy, whom we named Paul. Our cup was running over with joy. Since I had moved to Greenslopes specifically to complete my theological studies, it was unfortunate that Caroline was often left alone to bring up our three young children, but my pastoral duties helped me to support my family financially.

Students at the Baptist College were allocated to different local churches to further their experience in ministry, and a young lady called Sue Knott had been allocated to Greenslopes to minister the ladies as Caroline was indisposed, being responsible for the raising of our 3 young children. Sue was to prove herself a lifeline to Caroline during my many absences since she sacrificed her lunch hour to bring Caroline lunch and give her an adult to converse with, but Sue's main duties were full time within the ministry of the Church. She was a blessing.

I decided to do the Clinical Pastoral Course at the Wesley Hospital which I felt would enable me to be more helpful in my hospital visitations. Visiting the sick and the dying was something close to my heart. To sit holding the hand of a dying saint, and to witness their serenity as they faced their death was always a moving experience.

The College asked me to hold weekly services at Nursing Homes, and I always looked forward to these visits. The frailty of the residents always reminded me that there is a time for everything. "A time to be born and a time to die," and the time to die was quickly catching up with the aged residents I visited. I would always choose the old favourite hymns they knew and loved so well because my own spirit would lift in praise when I saw the joy on the faces of those who loved the Lord, but there was a sad side to my visits. There were residents slouched in their chairs oblivious to what was going on around them, seemingly abandoned and forgotten by their children; never ever getting a visit from them.

One of the most difficult duties I had was taking the funerals of a suicide which I have had to take a number of over the years. In the past, those that died by their own hand were denied a Christian burial, like Judas Iscariot they were cast away and buried in a potter's field away from the sanctified ground of a Christian cemetery. (Matt. 27:5-10). The intentional killing of oneself is a mortal sin. The Sixth

Commandment clearly states, "You shall not murder" (Exodus 20:13), and suicide in my eyes is murdering oneself. Yet, let us not be too hasty to judge.

A person who dies by his own hand can be struggling with some form of addiction or suffering a mental disorder or dealing with some deep and secret issues known only to themselves and to God. They can be desperately crying out for help and do not know which way to turn. There are those who are not in their right state of mind when making the decision to enact the taking of their own lives. God is a God of compassion and on Judgment Day, He will judge each case individually for He alone knows the heart of each of us.

With my theological studies completed and having graduated from the Baptist Theological College, I was happily settled in at Greenslopes Church as the Pastor. Church numbers had increased, and I was enjoying the friendliness of Greenslopes, but slowly our thoughts began to turn again to foreign missionary service. Caroline and I were both fluent in Spanish and we felt our language skills should be used again in some Spanish speaking country of the world.

My ministry at Greenslopes came to an end in 1983, after almost 4 happy years as Pastor of that community. On the Church's 100th Anniversary in 2021 a book had been published on its history from 1920 onwards. My time at the Church was defined as a time of numerical growth. It was a great honour and privilege to have served there. To this day we are still in contact with close friends that belong to the Greenslopes church.

Return to Mission Work

At the end of May Pastor Peter C. Horrell will conclude three years of ministry at the Greenslopes Baptist Church to begin preparations for his return to overseas missionary work.

Prior to his call to Greenslopes, Mr. Horrell served as interim pastor at the Townsville District Baptist Church.

For nearly ten years he served the Lord in South America, firstly in a fruitful church planting ministry in Colombia.

After marriage in 1973, Mr. and Mrs. Horrell went to Venezuela where they were engaged in a teaching ministry in a Bible College.

The Horrells and their three children plan to leave for Spain in June, 1984 for service with the Christian and Missionary Alliance of Australia.

Picture taken some time in 1983 just before we left for Spain

Me on a fishing trip in Brisbane, before leaving for Spain

Spain

There was an intermission of approximately a year before we actually left for Spain, during which time Caroline and I had joined the "Christian & Missionary Alliance," an American missionary society based in Sydney. I pastored an Alliance church in Sydney to get acquainted with the group, and after a few months I was moved to Melbourne with my family to pastor an Alliance church there. It was a hectic time for us all and in 1985, in preparation for our journey to Spain, we boarded a flight to the UK so that Caroline and the children could get know my sister (and their aunt) Freda, in Okehampton.

I travelled ahead to Spain to find accommodation in the city of Zaragoza where we had been assigned. Zaragoza is named after Julius Caesar and is midway between Barcelona and Madrid. I found and rented an apartment that would suit us, arranged for Caroline and the kids to fly over to Barcelona airport where I picked them up, and we then enrolled Peter-Andrew, Tania and Paul into the Colegio Britannica de Zaragoza that taught English to Spanish children. The ability to speak English was considered prestigious so there was a lot of jealousy directed towards Peter-Andrew, in particular, as a native English speaker needing to learn Spanish. He was in grade 3 which can be a difficult time for children if they're considered 'different' and, as a result, he was the butt of many childhood pranks that were sometimes very cruel.

After almost two years the Church leadership offered us a move to a place where there was an English-speaking school within the Church framework and we made the decision to move the family once again, back from Zaragoza to Barcelona so we could enrol the three of them into the American Alliance School. This decision was to improve the lives of all the kids but benefitted Peter-Andrew the most.

Caroline started an outreach program capitalizing on the Spanish custom of having coffee with friends after dropping off their children at school. She hired a restaurant once every three months whereby women could meet and listen to the testimonies of others speak about what Jesus had done for them. These meetings became very popular with about 80 to 100 attending each session. Caroline, being a musician, also introduced musical items into these meetings. She had a team of women from the church who were able to assist in organizing these events. Caroline's use of the Spanish language was learned from everyday social interactions with 'real' women in 'real' situations; my Spanish was learned from academic study of the bible in Spanish and from men. We all know what men teach each other when they are passing on the juicy bits of a language!

Pictures of Caroline taking her ministry in Spanish and conducting ladies morning tea.

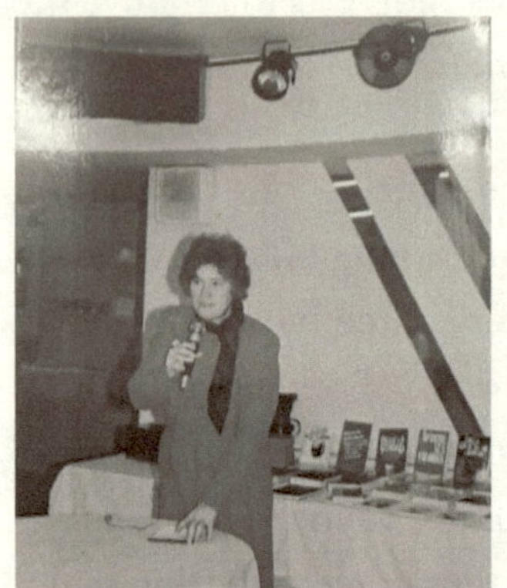

Caroline's Evangelistic Ministry Among Women

At this time, Caroline caught the underground train each week to a suburb outside of Barcelona to visit a friend's home to open God's word to a small group of housewives. She recalls the testimony of a Christian lady who had attended this Bible study during the dictatorship of Franco. The lady was with a group of girlfriends when the police suddenly arrived, disbanded the group, and arrested one of her friends whom they tortured to death. It left a deep scar in this lady's life. Her heart was reaching out for answers. She found them in the company of fellow Christians in the ladies group that Caroline had organized.

Caroline and I decided to spend one of our Christmas's with Freda in Okehampton, we had a Combi so we could do some camping as we made our way over to the UK. Crossing the English Channel by ferry, Peter Andrew began feeling unwell. As we travelled north, camping along the way to Nottingham, his condition worsened, and we had to call an ambulance. They rushed him to Nottingham University Hospital where they immediately operated on him for a burst appendix. We thought we were going to lose him; however, he slowly recovered and we continued to Okehampton and enjoyed our Christmas together.

Upon our return to Spain, Peter Andrew, by now 12 years of age, was ready to attend secondary school but this placed us in a dilemma. To have him educated him at a public school in the north of Spain, where we lived, meant he would have to be educated in Catalan. Catalan is a separate language to Spanish Castillano and is only spoken in northern Spain; nowhere else in the world is it found or spoken. The options before us were to send him to an International School in Germany, to send him to my sister Freda to be educated in England or, send him back to Australia where he would have to board with a Christian family. We didn't feel comfortable with any of these options. He was our son and our responsibility to bring up, so, we decided for the sake of his education we would return home to Australia.

Australia. Murgon Baptist Church

Upon our return to Australia, I was asked if I would pastor Murgon's Baptist Church. Murgon is a rural town in the South Burnett region with large piggery farms in the area, and some of their owners were members of my church. My visitation to its scattered membership covered a sizeable area of land that included these piggeries. Before entering a piggery, I would always take the biggest breath my lungs would take and hold it for as long as I could. "*My word,*" I once jokingly said to a farmer, *"how on earth are you able to put up with such a stench"* He cleared his throat, wiggled his nose, took two big sniffs and declared, "*What stench? The only stench I can smell are dollars.*"" Sometimes I took my children along with me and they always enjoyed these visits to the piggeries because it meant they were able to cuddle the piglets. Not my preference, but they loved it!

I confess I found it difficult to blend into Murgon's rural way of life. After the Sunday morning services, the men would gather in small groups and discuss the topics associated with their businesses and though I would always join them, I felt the odd man out. We had a visit from our Baptist evangelist, who, after his ministry with us quietly said, “Peter, Murgon is not your place”, which confirmed my own thoughts. After a year or so in Murgon, it was time for me to move on.

CALOUNDRA

I was invited by the Caloundra Baptist Church in the 1990's to join its team of three pastors, to make a team of four. It was a large Church with an estimated attendance of between five to six hundred at each of its services. I was enjoying my ministry there until, into my second year with the church rumours began circulating about an alleged relationship between the senior pastor and a few female members of the church, which eventually proved to be true. The two other pastors wanted to cover it up and say nothing, but I felt strongly I had to say something to the church.

On this particular Sunday morning the Caloundra church was packed and most of my congregation was aware that there was something terribly wrong with its leadership. In doing what I had to do, I knew that my time at this church was about to end. I walked up to the pulpit and simply said, *"This Church is going to pass through a terrible storm"*. I read from Ezekial 13; a passage that describes the actions of two false prophets and I told the congregation that they needed to pray in earnest. There was a silence. I stepped down and left the church and shortly after that my contract with the church was terminated by one of the other pastors.

As a result of the behaviour of that senior Pastor, this once thriving church lost nearly all its membership along with its teachers at the school, reduced from a ministry of almost 600, down to around 50 members. The senior pastor was found guilty of immorality and defrocked from the ministry. I feel the Baptist Union of Queensland at the time should have taken a stronger responsibility for the breakup of the church. The Union was slow, some said reluctant to get involved. There were many petitions sent by the church's' members to the General Superintendent complaining about the behaviour of the Pastor but these were ignored and left unanswered. I cannot help thinking that the reluctance was because of the ties of 'mateship' that the Superintendent had with the Pastor. We were living in the manse, a house that belongs to the church, with three fairly young children at the school also run by the church. After this incident, we were immediately evicted and had it not been for the mercy of God, we would have been left in a dire position – three children and nowhere to live. As it was, the house we owned in Mapleton, which had been rented out until the very week prior to this incident, suddenly became vacant.

Despite this turn of fortune, like the pilgrim in Bunyan's "Pilgrims Progress", I found myself sinking into a 'Slough of Despond'. I was physically, mentally and emotionally tired. I was asked to Pastor a church in Chinchilla, but I refused. My belief in church leadership had been shaken and had pushed me to the limit. Caroline took on a position as a telemarketer to help the family survive and later created her own business in this field which thrived!

Tasmania

A friend who lived in Railton, Tasmania heard about our situation and invited us to spend time with him. He was in contact with several different churches where he lived and where I was invited to speak. During the time we spent with him I must have spoken in just about every different denominational church in the area. At one stage I was encouraged by the Anglican Bishop of Tasmania to seek ordination within the Anglican Church. As a Baptist I couldn't see myself dressed in the vestments of a clergyman, using the Prayer Book, and prostrating myself before the Host.

Due to family matters at home, Caroline had to return to the mainland where our children had been staying, leaving me to fulfil other commitments already made. One of these was to house sit for a few days while the owner visited her family on the mainland as well. Her home was in the town of Sheffield, located in the foothills of the majestic Mount Roland, gateway to Cradle Mountain. Sheffield is where history and art merge to create an entire town of over 200 murals and her house was situated away from the township up close to the mountain. I had her two small dogs to look after but other than them I was in complete solitude, with only the sounds and beauty of nature around me, I was able to finally finish the manuscript of my book, "*The End Of Time – The Final Conflict'* based on the Book of Revelation. It was finally published by a London publisher in 2020.

Upon my return to the mainland, we had a visit from Fred & Moira Horrell, sheep farmers from New Zealand - I have already mentioned how I had received an aerogramme from Moira when I was in Colombia in the 70's. She told me her Presbyterian Church was without a pastor and asked me if I would consider the position. I was happy to do so.

New Zealand

The Horrell's were among the early settlers in New Zealand. "Horrellville", located in the Waimakariri District, Canterbury region, was named after the prominent early settler John Horrell in 1840. Caroline and I were to meet many of his descendants during our time over there. Moira's Presbyterian Church was in Tuatapere, a small rural town in the Southland and the self-declared "Sausage Capital" of New Zealand. We quickly settled into a church fellowship that felt like we were meeting family members and that was truly the case, for the Horrell family's roots go back hundreds of years to Okehampton in England.

Our time in New Zealand was most enjoyable. It was a pleasure to have been able to minister to them Sunday by Sunday, and to enjoy the church's picnics and outings we had together. Caroline started a woman's prayer and Bible study group that was well attended and a source of blessing to many. We had spent a little over a year with the Horrell family but the time came when we felt we needed to return to Australia and catch up with our own children, who were adults.

Australia

Upon our return the first thing that hit us was the stench, it was like walking into a brick wall. We discovered that our car which had been parked for over a year was infested with live and decomposing rats. The stench of the piggeries in Murgon smelt like perfume in comparison to the stench of those dead rodents. Settling into Maleny I joined the Maleny RSL Club and became its Chaplain. I couldn't help thinking that more than 50 years earlier I had been kicked out of an RSL Club for slighting the Queen.

Hospital

In 2014 I was diagnosed with microscopic polyangiitis, a rare type of vasculitis, which left me fighting for my life in an ICU in hospital in Caloundra. I was completely at peace, and ready, even looking forward, to being with Christ. I survived the illness with an insatiable urge to write. It was as if I felt my time was limited, I had been too close to my mortality. I lost interest in food and sleep; at times I found myself writing through the whole night. I completed a half-finished document that has now been published titled "*Reflections – Songs, Poetry and Meditations*". As mentioned earlier, I also wrote a book called "*The End Of Time – The Final Conflict*" based on the book of Revelation and the Old Testament prophets.

Then something occurred that left Caroline and I devastated and homeless. It came from our eldest son and his wife. They had bought our home in Maleny for half its value with the verbal agreement that we could stay there until we could no longer look after ourselves and must go into a nursing home. They went back on their word. They realised they could get more money by renting it out, so they left us out on the street. Though his betrayal cut deep we have forgiven him. Our love for him has never diminished.

And so, at the age of 90 as the story of my life comes to an end, I continue to write. Recently, I have had published the book *"Going Deeper With God"*, which is proving to be a blessing to many.

I recall the time more than 50 years ago when I climbed the slopes of Mt. Eden in New Zealand to spend time alone with God. I felt so close to Him that I wanted to remain forever on that mountain top, but my calling was to descend into the valley where the people lived without hope and without Christ. Now I face my last valley that I must pass through; the Valley of Death (Psalm 23). I have no fear of this Valley, indeed I long to pass through it to be forever with Jesus, who saved me and used me for His glory. I had a dream which impacted me strongly enough for me to recall it as the following poem;

The Valley was behind me, I had passed through the valley of death,
My earthly pilgrimage had ended when I took my final breath.
I was never alone in the Valley, for Jesus my Saviour was there,
He walked me through the Valley, secure in His loving care.

There was no fear of evil, no dread disturbed my peace,
His Presence ever with me, His love had never ceased.
We walked and talked together, oh! what joy His face to see,
And the glory of His Kingdom, He had prepared for me.

Oh! Christian friend, do not fear, you'll never walk alone,
Jesus, your Guide and Shepherd, will lead you safely home.
He'll guide you through the Valley, the Valley of your death,
And lead you to the place, of your eternal happiness.

My Testimony to God's Love

Many years ago, I walked past a broken-down hotel where I saw a man was leaning drunkenly against the bar. Thoughts from my own past came to mind. It was I whom I saw leaning against that bar, a spectre of my former self, a ghost from my distant past. That night, alone in my room, I thought back over my life and began to write:

It was I that was leaning against that bar,
A forlorn figure of satire;
My head was bowed, my heart did ache,
For drink my life did dominate;
The serpents bite within the brew
Had conquered my life, and *that* I knew.

I loathed myself, I'd lost my hold,
Over all I was and once controlled;
Shackled like slave to what I hate,
My silent prayer: 'O death me take'
But death ignored my supplication,
And joined the world in my rejection.

I walked alone, a soul abandoned,
The ghost of past memories my sole companion;
I recalled my childhood and my teens,
My days of innocence, my boyhood dreams;
Carefree I played with never a fear,
Cruel fate was mine to grow old in years.

Like Prodigal of old in squanderers living,
To pleasure and sin my life I'd given;
I'd travelled far to distant regions,
Gambled, drank and danced with demons;
In life of shame where ever I trod,
No thought for man, even less for God.

I knew it not but a chain I forged,
Each link a vice that enslaved my soul;
I drank my fill, had thrown the dice,
chained and mastered by my vice;
A captive led by sin's command,
Made a slave by my own hand.

I'd travelled far, in sin had wallowed,
But: "*The Hound of Heaven*"* my footsteps followed;
seized and smitten by His love divine,
Overpowered, He broke this heart of mine;
My God I cried: 'O set me free';
And His hand of love reached down to me.

Conquered, at last my life I gave,
A captive freed, yet a captive made;
He freed me from my chains of vice,
I'm still a slave, but the slave of Christ;
Held forever in God's embrace,
Forever imprisoned in His realm of grace.

Slowly I walked past that bar,
That solitary figure of satire;
O God I prayed: with your love divine,
Touch his heart as You touched mine;
Hastening on with quickened pace,
thought: "There go I but for God's grace".

P.C. Horrell

* *The "Hound of Heaven" refers to the Spirit of God*
Poem by Francis Thompson (1859-1907)

About The Author

Peter C. Horrell was born in England in 1936. He served in the British Army in Kenya in the mid-50s during the Mau Mau conflict. As a traveller and adventurer, he hiked around Europe, immigrated to Australia and later moved to New Zealand in the early 60's. In New Zealand he had, what he called, a "Damascus Road" encounter with Christ. He felt a call to foreign missionary service and spent time at the Missionary Training College in Tasmania where he met his future wife, Caroline. Together they served in South America and Spain. Upon their return to Australia, Peter completed his theological studies at the Baptist Theological College of Queensland. He has been a Baptist pastor of churches in Australia and New Zealand and has written several Christian articles including this autobiography. His interests are poetry, archaeology, early European history and succulent plants. He and his wife Caroline have retired and live in Maleny, Queensland, Australia. They have been married over 50 years and have 3 children.

His autobiography makes for extremely interesting reading. With a touch of humour, he openly and candidly shares his early life as an orphan, his time in the British army in Kenya, and his love for adventurous living. Ending up as a penniless drunk and a homeless derelict he was literally 'fished off' a street in Auckland, New Zealand. What followed reveals to us all what God can do with a life fully committed to Him. Read it. You will be blessed.

Graeme Cooksley
Queensland. Australia.

www.ingramcontent.com/pod-product-compliance
Lightning Source LLC
LaVergne TN
LVHW091012080826
845145LV00003B/1240